Need to improve your writing skills? F
in general?

This book will step you through different styles of writing.

Tips

- Plan- Who, what, when, where, why, how
- Use good vocabulary
- Keep it to the point⋯ don't ramble
- Check you have used VCOP- good vocabulary, good connectives, good openers and good punctuation.

Margins have been left in the book for you to plan and comments to be made.

Good luck!

Creative Writing 1. ✓
Should mobile phones be banned in schools?

- This is a debate style question.
- These debate style questions come often in private school exams.
- Start off with an introduction. Give a short insight into the topic, and link it to the question 'Should mobile phones be banned in schools?'
- The next paragraph should provide points with either for or against, but stick to one category. It is usually the category that you have stronger points for.
- Structure for the second and third paragraph should follow the acronym PEEL. Point, evidence, explanation, link back to the question. Following this structure will give you higher marks in the exam.
- The next paragraph should provide points contradicting your paragraph before. If you wrote some points for the argument in the previous paragraph, then write points against it in this one. Some good sentence starters include: On the other hand···, or however···.
- Finish off with a conclusion. Provide your final opinion here and explain as to why by giving the strongest point. This paragraph should be around the same size as the introduction, but about three lines longer.
- Now have a go at writing your debate.

_____

_____

_____

_____

_____

_____

_____

_____

√ 9/5/18

Magical Minds Learning © 2018

Creative Writing 2. ✓
Home Alone

You suddenly realise that you are on your own at your home. Write a diary entry accounting your time.

➤ Include your thoughts and feelings.
➤ Include lots of adjectives.

_____

_____

_____

_____

_____

_____

_____

_____

_____

_____

_____

_____

Activity ✓

Write a short description about the seaside.

➢ Make it as vivid as possible.
➢ Use adjectives
➢ Target- use a simile, metaphor and/or personification.
➢ Before you write – mind map some words and phrases below about the seaside that you can use in your writing. For example: How do the waves go? Calmly or roughly? Slowly or rapidly?

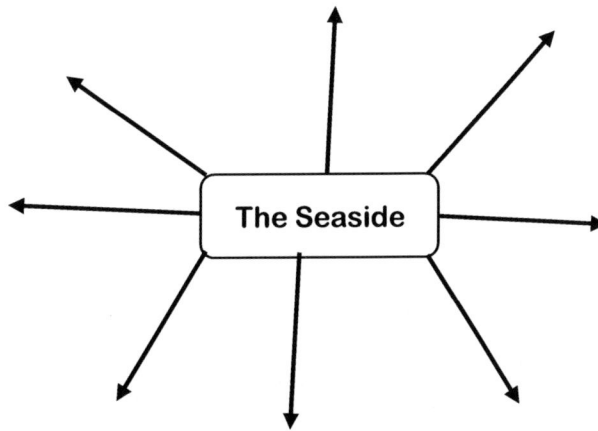

The Seaside

_____

_____

_____

_____

_____

_____

Creative Writing 3. ✓
Complaint Letter

You have just been to a restaurant and have had a very bad experience. Write a complaint letter to the restaurant manager.

- ➤ Keep it formal
- ➤ Plan ···

'Dear Sir/Madam,

I am writing to let you know about the execrable experience I had at your restaurant last Saturday.

First of all···

Secondly···

Finally···

Yours faithfully,'

_____

_____

_____

_____

_____

_____

_____

_____

_____

_____

_____

_____

_____

_____

_____

_____

_____

Creative Writing 4. ✓

'Museums are boring and old-fashioned.'
Do you agree with this statement?

➤ This is another debate style question.
➤ Start off with an introduction. Give a short insight into the topic, and link it to the statement 'Museums are boring and old fashioned.'
➤ The next paragraph should provide points with either for or against, but stick to one category. It is usually the category that you have stronger points for.
➤ Structure for the second and third paragraph should follow the acronym PEEL. Point, evidence, explanation, link back to the question. Following this structure will give you higher marks in the exam.
➤ The next paragraph should provide points contradicting your paragraph before. If you wrote some points for the argument in the previous paragraph, then write points against it in this one. Some good sentence starters include: On the other hand···, however···., others may argue···
➤ Finish off with a conclusion. Provide your final opinion here and explain as to why by giving the strongest point. This paragraph should be around the same size as the introduction, but about three lines longer.
➤ Now have a go at planning, then writing your debate.

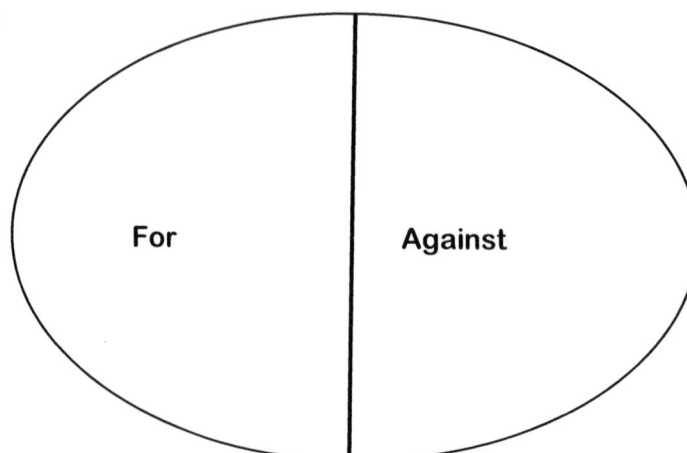

For   Against

_____

_____

Magical Minds Learning © 2018

Creative Writing 5. ✓

You have been given the starter of a short story. Continue it.

'My sister Emily and I absolutely love playing hide and seek. It's the suspense of being found, that I'm fond of... it is so exciting. Anyway, I now have to tell you a very thrilling story. Let me begin. Emily was counting. I couldn't find a place to hide, so I darted down the stairs and searched frantically around. It was then when I saw... '

> Use our planning guide to help you.

```
          ┌──────────────┐
          │   Place:      │
          └──────────────┘
┌──────────┐   ┌──────┐
│ What     │←──│ Plan │──→ ┌──────────┐
│ happens: │   └──────┘    │Characters:│
└──────────┘      │        └──────────┘
               ┌──────────┐
               │ Ending:  │
               └──────────┘
```

_____

_____

_____

_____

_____

_____

_____

_____

_____

_____

Activity ✓

➤ Write a description about the night.
➤ Plan before you write- what are your connotations with the word night?

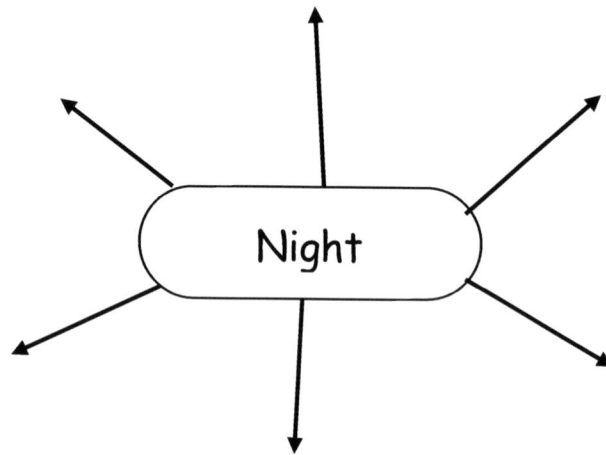

Night

_____

_____

_____

_____

_____

_____

_____

Creative Writing 6.
The Lost Thing.

Carry on the story-description.

'It was then when I saw it, nothing like I had ever seen before. I bent down to pick it up and I examined it carefully. Hmmm··· I said to myself··· That's very, very strange.'

Use this template to help you plan. We will look at a story mountain. You by all means do not have to stick to it, it just gives general idea of what a story as such should include.

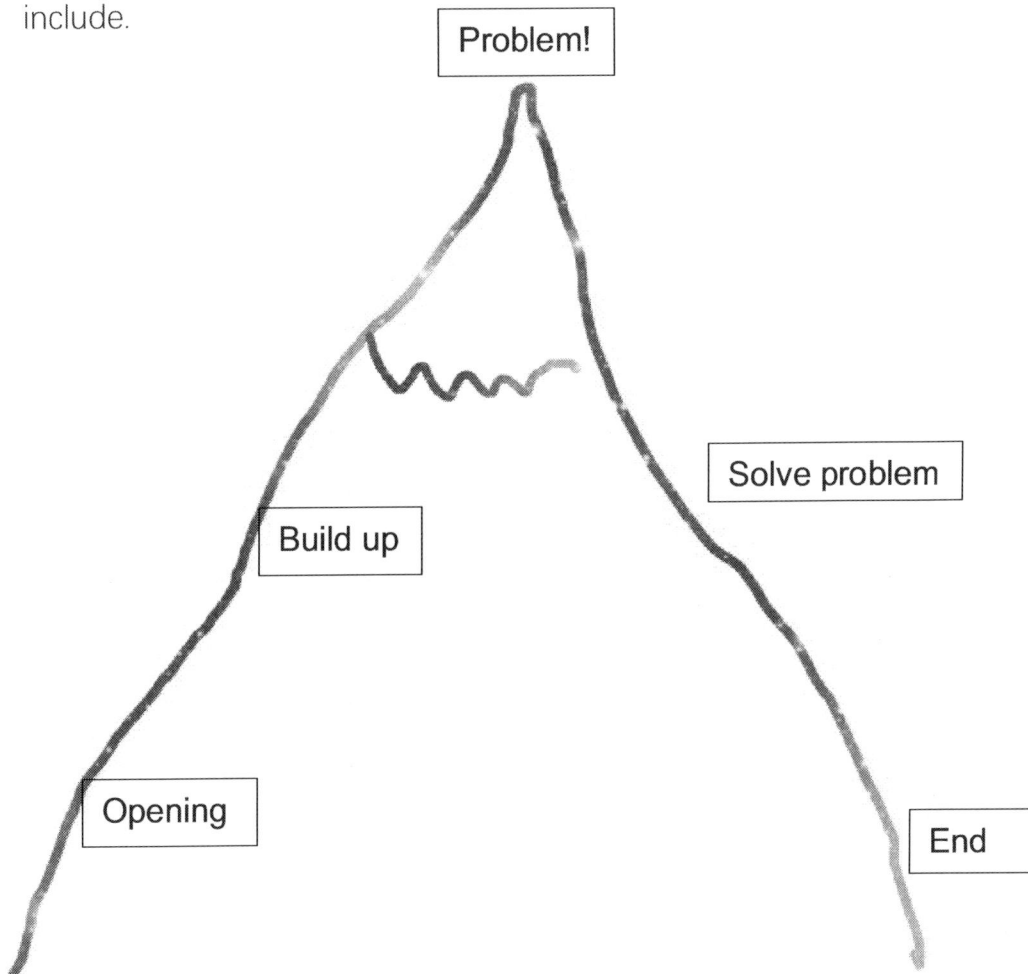

Problem!

Solve problem

Build up

Opening

End

_____

_____

_____

_____

_____

_____

_____

_____

_____

_____

_____

_____

_____

Magical Minds Learning © 2018

Creative Writing 7. ✓
Character description

Write a character description. It can be based on anything you want.
Make sure to use good vocabulary. Try to include a situation where the character's personality is revealed.

_____

_____

_____

_____

_____

_____

_____

_____

_____

_____

_____

_____

_____

_____

_____

Activity

Carry on the paragraph…

'The hustle and bustle of the street was too much for me to handle. I put my hand in my pocket and realised that my wallet was missing.'

_____

_____

_____

_____

_____

_____

_____

_____

_____

_____

_____

_____

_____

_____

Do you keep on repeating the word said? Fear not, we have a handy little list for you, with other words you can use for said (use different contexts).

1. Replied
2. Exclaimed
3. Queried
4. Questioned
5. Murmured
6. Muttered
7. Screamed
8. Shouted
9. Whispered
10. Laughed
11. Cried
12. Whined
13. Yelled
14. Encouraged
15. Answered
16. Complained
17. Taunted
18. Whimpered
19. Barked
20. Giggled
21. Ordered
22. Implored
23. Insisted
24. Interrupted

25. Bellowed
26. Mimicked
27. Uttered
28. Objected
29. Observed
30. Offered
31. Cowered
32. Sneered
33. Snarled
34. Remembered
35. Lied
36. Exaggerated
37. Cackled
38. Squealed
39. Demanded
40. Sobbed
41. Hollered
42. Persisted
43. Pestered
44. Pleaded
45. Pondered
46. Prattled
47. Prayed
48. Proclaimed
49. Proposed
50. Protested
51. Snapped
52. Advised
53. Added

Creative Writing 8.
Should homework be voluntary?

> ➤ This is a debate style question.
> ➤ Start off with an introduction. Give a short insight into the topic, and link it to the question 'Should homework be voluntary?'
> ➤ The next paragraph should provide points with either for or against, but stick to one category. It is usually the category that you have stronger points for.
> ➤ Structure for the second and third paragraphs should follow the acronym PEEL. Point, evidence, explanation, link back to the question. Following this structure will give you higher marks in the exam.
> ➤ The next paragraph should provide points contradicting your paragraph before. If you wrote some points for the argument in the previous paragraph, then write points against it in this one. Some good sentence starters include: On the other hand···, or however···.
> ➤ Finish off with a conclusion. Provide your final opinion here and explain as to why by giving the strongest point. This paragraph should be around the same size as the introduction, but about three lines longer.
> ➤ Now have a go at writing your debate.

_____

_____

_____

_____

_____

_____

_____

_____

Creative Writing 9.
<u>Should students have to wear school uniform?</u>

- ➤ This is a debate style question.
- ➤ Start off with an introduction. Give a short insight into the topic, and link it to the question 'Should students have to wear school uniform?'
- ➤ The next paragraph should provide points with either for or against, but stick to one category. It is usually the category that you have stronger points for.
- ➤ Structure for the second and third paragraphs should follow the acronym PEEL. Point, evidence, explanation, link back to the question. Following this structure will give you higher marks in the exam.
- ➤ The next paragraph should provide points contradicting your paragraph before. If you wrote some points for the argument in the previous paragraph, then write points against it in this one. Some good sentence starters include: On the other hand···, or however···.
- ➤ Finish off with a conclusion. Provide your final opinion here and explain as to why by giving the strongest point. This paragraph should be around the same size as the introduction, but about three lines longer.
- ➤ Now have a go at writing your debate.

_____

_____

_____

_____

_____

_____

_____

_____

_____

Activity. ✓

What are you favourite memories?

➤ Write a description about your favourite memories. They can be real or from your imagination .

_____

_____

_____

_____

_____

_____

_____

_____

_____

_____

_____

_____

_____

_____

_____

Magical Minds Learning © 2018

Creative Writing 10.
Continue the story.

It's the middle of the night.

I amble along Lemon's Avenue, coming home from a late shift at the shop. The road is empty and it's ever so dark, but I keep my head held high and carry on walking. I don't get scared! Maybe I should have kept my old job at the aquarium, then I would have now been snuggled up in the warmth of my bed. Oh well, I might as well just be optimistic and be grateful that I get a higher pay in my new job as manager at Greenacre shop. Having the feeling that somebody is following me, I look around gingerly, however no one is there.

The air feels icy and cold, I up my walking pace- a shiver goes down my spine. I daren't search to see if anyone is in the streets. After all, it is the middle of the night. Anything could happen.

Out of the blue, I hear a noise. A deafening noise, like a scream. Who could it be? I run while my heart pounds. When I reach my house I fumble around in my rucksack for my keys to open the door.

_____

_____

_____

_____

_____

_____

_____

_____

Creative Writing 11.

Now you've had practice with creative writing, <u>write a short story</u>. It can be about anything you want..

➤ Identify the genre.
➤ Identify the mood.
➤ Plan, plan, plan!
➤ You can plan in anyway you like.. the story mountain, annotations.

_____

_____

_____

_____

_____

_____

_____

_____

_____

_____

_____

_____

_____

_____

Creative Writing 12. ✓

Write a short story about moving houses.

- ➢ Characters
- ➢ Place
- ➢ When
- ➢ Why
- ➢ How do you/they feel?

_____

_____

_____

_____

_____

_____

_____

_____

_____

_____

_____

_____

_____

Printed in Great Britain
by Amazon